THE POCKET GUIDE TO BRIDGE

BARBARA SEAGRAM • RAY LEE

D0754170

Master Point Press

331 Douglas Ave.
Toronto, Ontario Canada
M5M 1H2
(416) 781-0351
Internet www.masterpointpress.com

Canadian Cataloguing in Publication Data

Barbara Seagram
The pocket guide to bridge
ISBN 1-894154-41-X
1. Contract bridge. I. Ray Lee, 1945 II. Title.
GV1282.3.S42 2002   795.41'5   C2001-904145-4

Cover and Interior design Olena S. Sullivan/New Mediatrix
Interior format and copyediting Deanna Bourassa

Printed and bound in Canada by Webcom
7 8 9 10 11   16 15 14 13 12

CONTENTS

1. HOW GOOD IS YOUR HAND?

To answer this question, you need to consider two aspects of your hand:

high cards *and* **distribution**

COUNTING POINTS

Count the **high card points** (HCP) in your hand using the following table:

> *Ace = 4*
> *King = 3*
> *Queen = 2*
> *Jack = 1*

A shortcut: 'The Royal Family'
A + K + Q + J = 10

There are two ways to count your **distributional points**; both work, so don't worry which one you use, or even if you use one and your partner uses the other:

Method 1: count long suits

1 point for the fifth card in a suit
1 more point for any card after the fifth

Method 2: count short suits

> *Void = 3*
> *Singleton = 2*
> *Doubleton = 1*

Do not count short suit points for unprotected honors, which can be 'eaten up' by higher honors. So count no distributional points for

> *Singleton K*
> *Doubleton or singleton Q*
> *Tripleton, doubleton or singleton J*

Add your HCP to your distributional points to get the **total points**.

Here are some examples of how counting your total points works:

♠ A K J 8 6	HCP = 14
♡ Q 10 8	Dist. = 1
◇ A 4 2	Total = 15
♣ 6 4	

♠ A K 8	HCP = 12
♡ A J 9 7 5 4 3	Dist. = 3
◇ 4 2	Total = 15
♣ 6	

♠ A J 8	HCP = 13
♡ 2	Dist. = 2
◇ A K 4	Total = 15
♣ J 10 9 7 5 3	

Distributional points are only useful if you are going to play a trump contract, when your short suits may enable you to score some tricks by ruffing. If you are going to play in notrump, count only HCP; if you are considering a trump contract, use total points to value your hand.

WHY YOUR POINT COUNT CAN CHANGE

As the bidding progresses, you need to revalue your hand. The following rules can be used:

- If you have four or more cards in a suit partner has bid, you will likely be the dummy. Start fresh, and this time count **dummy points** as follows:

    void = 5
    singleton = 3
    doubleton = 1

Add these to your HCP.

♠ A 7 6 3	
♡ 6	HCP = 8
◇ A 4 3 2	Dist. = 3
♣ 5 4 3 2	Total = 11

On this hand, if partner opens the bidding 1♠, you can add 3 dummy points to your 8 HCP for a total of 11.

- When partner has supported your suit, suggesting that it will probably be trumps, then reevaluate your distributional points as follows:

Add 1 point for the fifth card in a suit
Add 2 points for the sixth and each subsequent card in a suit
Add points for shortness as follows:

> *Void= 3 points*
> *Singleton= 2 points*
> *Doubleton = 1 point*

However, never count distribution points for shortness in partner's suits. This is *never* an asset.

Notice that it doesn't matter whether the first time round you counted long suits or short suits — once you have found a trump fit, everyone counts the same way!

♠ A J 8	(first count)
♡ 6	HCP = 13
◇ A K 4	Dist. = 2
♣ J 10 9 7 5 3	Total = 15

If partner supports your clubs, count 3 for the 5th and 6th clubs and 2 for the singleton heart, and revalue the hand to 18 points.

♠ A K 8	(first count)
♡ A J 9 7 5 4 3	HCP = 12
◇ 4 2	Dist. = 3
♣ 6	Total = 15

If partner raises hearts, count 2 for your singleton, 1 for your doubleton, and 5 for your 5th, 6th and 7th hearts. This revalues the hand up to 20 points!

♠ A K J 8 6	(first count)
♡ Q 10 8	HCP = 14
◇ A 4 2	Dist. = 1
♣ 6 4	Total = 15

If partner raises spades, count 1 for the 5th spade and 1 for the doubleton, for a total of 16 points.

USING POINT COUNT

There are two main ways to use your point count total: deciding whether to open the bidding, and determining what level contract you and your partner should try for.

Note: from here on, we shall let you calculate the total points in a hand for yourself.

To open the bidding you need 13 total points (HCP + distribution)

♠ A J 8	HCP = 13
♡ —	Dist. = __
◊ A K 4 2	Total = __
♣ J 10 9 7 5 3	

On this hand you may open the bidding.

♠ K J 8 6 4	HCP = 9
♡ K Q 10 8 4	Dist. = __
◊ 4 2	Total = __
♣ 6	

This hand is not good enough to open the bidding, but you will probably get to make a bid at some stage.

Number of points in combined hands to produce a given number of tricks

Total points	Tricks	Possible contracts
20	8	2♣, 2◊, 2♡, 2♠
23	9	3♣, 3◊, 3♡, 3♠
26	10	4♣, 4◊, 4♡, 4♠
29	11	5♣, 5◊, 5♡, 5♠
33	12	6♣, 6◊, 6♡, 6♠
37	13	7♣, 7◊, 7♡, 7♠

High card points	Tricks	Possible contracts
20	7	1NT
23	8	2NT
25	9	3NT
33	12	6NT
37	13	7NT

Some players follow the **Rule of 20**, in which you add your HCP to the lengths of your two longest suits. If this totals 20 or more, you may open the bidding.

2. OPENING ONE OF A SUIT

Opening hands can be divided into three types (minimum, promising, and strong), and are classified as either balanced or unbalanced. The definitions of these are:

13-15 points	**minimum**
16-18 points	**promising**
19+ points	**strong**

If you look at these in the light of the combined point count table on p.7, you can see the real meaning of these categories:

Minimum: you'll need something close to an opening bid from partner to make a game.

Promising: you have about one trick more than a basic opener, and may be able to make game opposite a moderate hand.

Strong: you need very little from partner to make a game, and may easily be in the slam zone.

*A **balanced** hand is a hand with no singletons or voids, and no more than one doubleton.*

♠ A Q J 8	HCP = 14
♡ K 10 8 4	Dist. = __
◇ A 4 2	Total = __
♣ 6 3	*Minimum, balanced*

♠ A K Q 8	HCP = 15
♡ Q 10 8 4	Dist. = __
◇ A 4 2	Total = __
♣ 6 3	*Promising, balanced*

♠ A Q 8	HCP = 14
♡ —	Dist. = __
◇ A K 4 2	Total = __
♣ J 10 9 7 5 3	*Promising, unbalanced*

♠ A K J 8 6	HCP = 17
♡ A K Q 10 8	Dist. = __
◇ 4 2	Total = __
♣ 6	*Strong, unbalanced*

CHOOSING AN OPENING BID

Two special types of hands are discussed in later sections. These are:

15-17 balanced	*Open 1NT (see p. 25)*
20+ HCP	*Open 2NT, 3NT or 2♣*
	(see pp. 25 and 37)

All other hands with at least 13 points are opened 1♣, 1◇, 1♡ or 1♠.

Which suit do you open?

* *Open your longest suit that is at least five cards in length.*
* *With two five-card suits or six-card suits, open the higher-ranking one*
* *With no five-card or longer suit, open your longer minor*
* *with two four-card minors, open 1◇*
* *with two three-card minors, open 1♣*

In the early days of bridge, many people felt that a suit had to contain a certain number of honor cards to be a 'biddable' suit; unless it did, you were not allowed to bid it unless your partner introduced it first. The modern style is to regard any four-card suit, even one such as ◇ 5 4 3 2 , as 'biddable', and in certain circumstances you are even allowed to bid a three-card suit. Any five-card suit is *rebiddable,* meaning you may bid it more than once. There are, however, some rules regarding opening bids and suit length. If you do not follow these, you are going to have some very surprised partners!

1. *Do not open 1♠ or 1♡ without at least five cards in your suit.*
2. *Do not open 1♣ or 1◇ without at least three cards in your suit.*

♠ A K Q 8 6	HCP = 15
♡ Q 10 8 4	Dist. = __
◇ A 4 2	Total = __
♣ 6	Unbalanced

Open 1♠ (longest suit)

♠ A K J 8	HCP = 15
♡ K 10 8 4	Dist. = __
◇ A 4 2	Total = __
♣ 6 3	Balanced

Open 1NT (15-17 HCP, balanced)

♠ A J 8	HCP = 13
♡ —	Dist. = __
◇ A K 4 2	Total = __
♣ J 10 9 7 5 3	Unbalanced

Open 1♣ (longest suit)

♠ A K J 8 6	HCP = 17
♡ A K Q 10 8	Dist. = __
◇ 4 2	Total = __
♣ 6	Unbalanced

Open 1♠ (higher-ranking 5-card suit)

♠ A Q 8 6	HCP = 13
♡ Q 10 8 4	Dist. = __
◇ A J 2	Total = __
♣ 6 3	Balanced

Open 1◇ (longer minor, no 5-card suit)

♠ A Q J 8	HCP = 14
♡ K 10 8	Dist. = __
◇ A 5 4 2	Total = __
♣ 6 3	Balanced

Open 1◇ (longer minor, no 5-card suit)

♠ A J 8	HCP = 14
♡ —	Dist. = __
◇ 8 7 5 4 2	Total = __
♣ A K Q 5 3	Unbalanced

Open 1◇ (higher-ranking 5-card suit)

♠ A K J 8 6	HCP = 16
♡ A K J 10 8 5	Dist. = __
◇ 4	Total = __
♣ 6	Unbalanced

Open 1♡ (longest suit)

♠ A K 8 6	HCP = 13		♠ A K Q J 6	HCP = 20
♡ J 10 8	Dist. = __		♡ 10	Dist. = __
◇ A 4 2	Total = __		◇ A K Q J 10	Total = __
♣ J 8 6	Balanced		♣ 9 8	Unbalanced

Open 1♣ (two 3-card minors)

Open 2♣ (very strong hand)

♠ Q 8 5	HCP = 13		♠ K Q 8 5	HCP = 19
♡ 8 4	Dist. = __		♡ K 4	Dist. = __
◇ A 5 4 2	Total = __		◇ A 5 4 2	Total = __
♣ A K 6 3	Balanced		♣ A K 6	Balanced

Open 1◇ (two 4-card minors)

Open 1◇ (too strong for 1NT)

♠ A J 8 6 3	HCP = 10		♠ A K 8 6 3	HCP = 11
♡ 6	Dist. = __		♡ K 6	Dist. = __
◇ A	Total = __		◇ 9 6 3	Total = __
♣ J 10 9 7 5 2	Unbalanced		♣ J 10 9	Balanced

Open 1♣ (longest suit)

Do not open (less than 13 points)

♠ A K J 8 6	HCP = 17		♠ A K Q J	HCP = 14
♡ 4	Dist. = __		♡ 6 4	Dist. = __
◇ 4 2	Total = __		◇ A 2	Total = __
♣ A K Q 10 8	Unbalanced		♣ 10 9 8 5 3	Unbalanced

Open 1♠ (higher-ranking suit)

Open 1♣ (longest suit)

RESPONDING TO AN OPENING SUIT BID

Again, it is helpful to divide your possible hands by point ranges. The first one is easy:

0-5 points Pass. Do not bid. This rule applies no matter what your distribution, and no matter how many or how few cards you have in partner's bid suit.

6-9 points You are going to take one bid, and one bid only, unless partner makes you bid again. You must therefore choose that one bid carefully and make it the most descriptive bid you can find.

We need one more definition before giving responder's rules: *trump support*, or put more simply, *do you like partner's suit?*

Adequate trump support (ATS) is three cards headed by an honor. If partner has shown a five-card suit, then ATS is any three cards.

Excellent trump support (ETS) is any four cards.

Responding with 6-9 points

- With at least ATS for partner's major, raise from 1 to 2 (*limited, non-forcing*). With 6-9 points and 5 trumps, raise partner's major to game immediately (e.g. 1♠ - 4♠).
- Bid your longest suit at the one-level (*unlimited, forcing*). Note: 1) you may not bid a new suit at the two-level, for this promises at least 10 points; 2) with two or more 4-card suits, bid the cheapest.
- Bid 1NT (*limited, non-forcing*). Note: this is the only notrump bid that does not promise a balanced hand.
- If no better bid is available, and you have ETS and a short suit, raise partner's minor from 1 to 2 (*limited, non-forcing*)

Apply these rules in strict order, using the first one that applies to your hand. Notice this means that if you raise partner's minor, you are denying a major suit of your own. You should bid 1NT instead of raising a minor unless you have a short suit somewhere.

Partner opens	*You respond*		
1♣ or 1♢	1♡	♠ A J 7 2	HCP = 6
1♡	2♡	♡ J 8 6 4	Dist. = __
1♠	2♠	♢ 6 2	Total = __
		♣ 10 9 8	Balanced
1♣ or 1♢	1NT	♠ Q 10 7	HCP = 6
1♡	2♡	♡ J 3 2	Dist. = __
1♠	2♠	♢ K 6 2	Total = __
		♣ 10 9 8 5	Balanced
1♢	2♢	♠ A 9	HCP = 5
1♣	2♣	♡ 6 4	Dist. = __
1♡ or 1♠	1NT	♢ J 6 4 2	Total = __
		♣ 10 9 8 6 3	Unbalanced
1♣ or 1♢	1♡	♠ A 10 7 2	HCP = 6
1♡	4♡	♡ Q 9 8 6 4	Dist. = __
1♠	2♠	♢ 4 2	Total = __
		♣ 7 5	Unbalanced
1♣ or 1♢	1♡	♠ 10 7	HCP = 7
1♡	4♡	♡ A K 7 6 4	Dist. = __
1♠	1NT	♢ 8 2	Total = __
		♣ 10 9 8 2	Unbalanced

Responding with 10-12 points

This is a hand in the *invitational* range — you want to invite partner to bid a game with more than a minimum opener. You need to convey this message, while at the same time exploring for a trump fit or suggesting notrump as a possible contract. Use these rules in order from the top until you find one that fits your hand.

- With ETS for partner's major, jump raise to the three-level (e.g. 1♠ — 3♠) — *limited, non-forcing*. If the opponents bid, you may jump raise with ATS.
- If partner has not bid a major, or if you have no support for partner's major, you will bid twice:

  1. First bid your longest suit (you may go to the two-level to do this if necessary)

  2. On your second turn, support partner if you can, otherwise bid naturally — rebid your suit, bid another new suit, or bid notrump at the lowest level you can.

- If no better bid is available you may jump raise partner's minor (need at least four).

```
HCP = 10        ♠ A J 7 2
Dist. = __      ♡ 6 4
Total = __      ◇ J 3 2
Balanced        ♣ A 9 8 5
```

Some possible auctions:

Partner	You
1♠	3♠

Partner	You
1♡	1♠
2◇	2NT

Partner	You
1♣	1♠
2♣	3♣

This shows the same strength as an initial raise to 3♣, but you always show your major before raising a minor.

Partner	You
1◇	1♠
2◇	3◇

Now partner has shown five diamonds, you can raise. You cannot bid 2NT with no heart stopper.

HCP = 11	♠ A J 2
Dist. = __	♡ A J 9 6 4
Total = __	◇ J 3 2
Balanced	♣ 8 5

Some possible auctions:

Partner	You
1♠	2♡
2♠	3♠

This shows the same strength as an initial raise to 3♠, but with only three trumps.

Partner	You
1◇	1♡
2♣	2NT

Partner	You
1♣	1♡
1NT[1]	2NT

1. Minimum hand, balanced.

Your 2NT invites partner to bid game with a hand at the top of the range.

HCP = 11	♠ Q 5 2
Dist. = __	♡ J 9 6 4
Total = __	◇ 3 2
Balanced	♣ A K 9 8

Some possible auctions:

Partner	You
1♡	3♡

Partner will bid game with a maximum.

Partner	You
1◇	1♡
2♡	2NT

With four hearts, partner will bid either 3♡ or 4♡ now. If partner has raised on three hearts, she will pass 2NT or raise you to 3NT.

Partner	You
1♠	2♣
2◇	2♠

There is no need to leap to 3♠ to show your values — partner knows you have at least 10 points from your 2♣ bid.

Responding with 13-15 points

As a rule, with an opening bid opposite an opening bid, you want to play in a game contract (there are rare exceptions). So when partner opens, you should:

• Bid a new suit and be responsible for getting your side to a game contract.

Remember that when responder bids a new suit, it is 100% forcing — *opening bidder may not pass*. It is also *unlimited* — you might make the same first response with a 6-9 point hand or with something much stronger; the fact that you keep bidding will tell partner you have a good hand.

Bid your longest suit first, going to the two-level if necessary to do so. If you have two or more four-card suits, bid the cheapest first, since this leaves more room. With two five-card suits you intend to bid both, so bid the higher-ranking first.

• With a balanced hand, no four-card major, no support for partner's major, stoppers in all unbid suits, and 13-15 HCP, bid 2NT — limited and forcing.

HCP = 12	♠ Q 3 2
Dist. = __	♡ K 9 6 4
Total = __	◇ 3
Unbalanced	♣ A K 9 8 5

Some possible auctions:

Partner	You
1♡	2♣
2◇	4♡

Partner	You
1♠	2♣
2◇	4♠

Partner	You
1◇	2♣
2◇	2♡
2NT	3NT

With 13-15 points, responder *must* make sure his side gets to game.

HCP = 11	♠ Q J 5 4 2
Dist. = __	♡ K J 9 6 4
Total = __	◇ 3
Unbalanced	♣ A 5

Some possible auctions:

Partner	You
1♣	1♠
2♣	2♡
2♠	4♠

Bid game once partner supports one of your suits.

Partner	You
1♣	1♠
2♣	2♡
2NT	3♡
4♡	

Bidding your suits this way guarantees at least five of each.

Partner	You
1◇	1♠
2♣	2♡
3♡	4♡

HCP = 13	♠ K 2
Dist. = __	♡ A J 9 6
Total = __	◇ Q 5 3 2
Balanced	♣ K 9 8

Some possible auctions:

Partner	You
1♣	1◇
1♠	3NT

Partner cannot have four hearts.

Partner	You
1◇	1♡
1NT[1]	3NT
1. Minimum, balanced.	

Partner	You
1♠	2NT

Bidding 2♡ over 1♠ always promises a five-card suit. You could bid 2◇, but 2NT describes your hand accurately in one bid.

Partner	You
1♡	2◇
2♡	4♡

Responding with strong hands

16-18 points: Your options here are similar to those for 13-15 point hands, but you need to convey your extra strength, often by trying to keep the auction open. A direct 3NT response shows a balanced 16-18 HCP, and denies either a major of your own or support for partner's major.

19+ points: *Jump shift* — bid your own 5-card suit a level higher than you have to, forcing to game. Thereafter, you can bid slowly and naturally, unafraid that partner will pass below game. You are very likely to be able to make a slam, so be alive to the possibilities.

These auctions are difficult to give rules for, since they develop over several rounds of bidding, and the number of possible bids by both partners is very large. The important thing is to understand which bids are forcing and which are not, as well as which bids limit your hand as responder, and which are forward-going.

HCP = 17	♠ A 2
Dist. = __	♡ A J 9
Total = __	◇ K 9 8
Balanced	♣ K Q 9 3 2

Some possible auctions:

Partner	You
1♡	2♣
2◇	3♡

With 10-12 you would bid 2♡ at your second turn and with 13-15 you would first bid 2♣ and then raise to 4♡. Here, the jump to 3♡ after your initial two-level response is forcing, and shows extra values and slam interest.

Partner	You
1♠	3NT

When you can describe your hand in one bid, do so. You have no spade support, no major of your own, and a balanced hand in the 16-18 HCP range. That's what your 3NT bid tells partner! Notice the difference from the previous auction, where you have some support for partner's major.

HCP = 15	♠ Q 3 2
Dist. = __	♡ A K J 9 6
Total = __	◇ K Q 5 3
Unbalanced	♣ 9

A possible auction:

Partner	You
1♠	2♡
2♠	3◇
3NT	4♠

Here you have bid two suits, and only then raised spades. Clearly you could have supported spades earlier, on the second round, which is what you would do with a 13-15 hand. This hand is in a stronger category, and opposite a partner who could open the bidding, you are permitted to have dreams of a slam. By bidding two new suits first and then bidding game in partner's major, you promise a hand in the 16-18 range. Partner can now revalue, and make a decision as to whether to make a move onwards.

HCP = 18	♠ Q 4 3
Dist. = __	♡ K J 2
Total = __	◇ A K J 9 6
Balanced	♣ A 2

Some possible auctions:

Partner	You
1♠	3◇
3♠	4♠

It is up to partner to move over 4♠. If he has a minimum opener and does not bid on, you do not want to be in a slam — he already knows you have a very strong hand.

Partner	You
1♣	2◇
3◇	3NT
6◇	

Again, having jump-shifted to begin the auction, you can afford to make a quiet descriptive bid over 3◇. If partner passes, you will be in the right spot. However, here partner knows about your strength and your good diamond suit, and that's enough for him to jump to 6◇.

REBIDS BY OPENING BIDDER

Again, we divide up hands according to strength:

13-15 points	**Minimum**
16-18 points	**Extra values**
19+ points	**Game-going**

With 13-15 points

Choose from these options; note that some choices limit your hand immediately, which is good, while others do not yet do so.

- Rebid your own suit at the cheapest level (must have at least five of them) — *13-15, non-forcing*

You	Partner
1◇	1♠
2◇	

- Raise partner's suit one level (need ATS) — *13-15, non-forcing*

You	Partner
1◇	1♠
2♠	

- Bid notrump at the cheapest level (with a balanced hand) — *12-14 HCP, non-forcing*

You	Partner
1◇	1♠
1NT	

You	Partner
1◇	2♣
2NT	

- Bid a new suit at the one-level — *non-forcing*

You	Partner
1◇	1♡
1♠	

- Bid a new, **lower-ranking** suit at the two-level — *non-forcing*

You	Partner
1◇	1♠
2♣	

In these last two auctions, you could have as much as 18 points and make the same bid. Nevertheless, partner can pass with a minimum (6 points) if she likes your second suit better.

♠ J 4 3	HCP = 13
♡ 4	Dist. = __
◇ A K J 9 6	Total = __
♣ A 4 3 2	Unbalanced

Some possible auctions:

You	Partner
1◇	1♡
2♣	

You	Partner
1◇	1♠
2♠	

You	Partner
1◇	2♣
3♣	

You	Partner
1◇	1NT
2♣	

Simple is best each time here. In the last three cases, your hand is quickly limited to at most 15 points.

♠ A K 5 3	HCP = 12
♡ A J 7 4 2	Dist. = __
◇ 4 2	Total = __
♣ 9 6	Unbalanced

You	Partner
1♡	2♣
2♡	

You are not strong enough to bid 2♠, which would show 17+ (see p.23), and an unbalanced hand may not rebid notrump.

♠ Q 2	HCP = 13
♡ A K 4	Dist. = __
◇ J 3 2	Total = __
♣ K 9 6 4 2	Balanced

You	Partner
1♣	1◇
1NT	

Rebidding a minor suit usually shows six cards. It is always preferable to rebid notrump if you can.

With 16-18 points

There are four options available to you:

- With a six-card suit of your own, jump rebid it.

You	Partner
1◇	1♠
3◇	

Partner should try to raise, or bid 3NT knowing your diamonds will likely be worth six tricks.

- With ETS for responder's suit, jump raise.

You	Partner
1◇	1♠
3♠	

Partner should bid 4♠ with a maximum (8-9) and pass with a minimum (6-7).

- Invite to game over a raise.

You	Partner
1♡	2♡
3♡	

You are asking partner to bid 4♡ with a maximum (8-9) and pass with a minimum (6-7).

- Rebid a second suit that is higher-ranking than your first. This promises 17+ points, and the first-bid suit must be longer than the second. This is called a **reverse** (because you reverse the usual order of bidding your suits). You need to have more strength because if partner likes your first suit better, you are going to be playing at the 3-level, not the 2-level.

♠ K 5	You	Partner
♡ A Q 4 2	1◇	1♠
◇ A K 10 8 4	2♡	
♣ 5 3		

You have 17 points and longer diamonds than hearts. Notice if partner likes diamonds better than hearts, you are going to be playing in 3◇, not 2◇. Compare the 'normal' order:

♠ K 5	You	Partner
♡ A 9 5 4 2	1♡	1♠
◇ A K 10 4	2◇	
♣ 5 3		

where if partner prefers your first suit, there is

no need to raise the level of the contract to return to it — he can simply bid 2♡. By contrast, since you will need to be able to stand playing in your first suit at the three-level, you need a stronger than minimum hand to use a reverse sequence.

♠ K 4 3 2	HCP = 15
♡ 4	Dist. = __
◇ A K J 9 6	Total = __
♣ A 4 3	Unbalanced

Some possible auctions:

You	Partner
1◇	1♡
1♠	2NT
3NT	

You	Partner
1◇	1♠
3♠	

♠ A 4 3	HCP = 16
♡ 4	Dist. = __
◇ A K J 9 6 2	Total __
♣ A 4 3	Unbalanced

Some possible auctions:

You	Partner
1◇	1♡
3◇	4◇
5◇	

You	Partner
1◇	1♠
3◇	3NT

♠ A K 10 4 3	HCP = 15
♡ 4	Dist. = __
◇ A 6 3 2	Total = __
♣ A 4 3	Unbalanced

You	Partner
1♠	2♠
3♠	

With 19+ points

Now your hand is so strong that once partner can respond to your opening bid, you want to be in game. You must get this message across immediately, and there are three ways to do this.

- With ETS in partner's major suit, bid game.

♠ A K J 4	HCP = 18
♡ 4 2	Dist. = __
◇ A Q 3 2	Total = __
♣ A 4 3	Balanced

You	**Partner**
1◇	1♠
4♠	

- With 18-19 HCP, a balanced hand, and stoppers in all the unbid suits, jump in notrump.

♠ A K J 4	HCP = 18
♡ 4 2	Dist. = __
◇ A Q 3 2	Total = __
♣ A 4 3	Balanced

You	**Partner**
1◇	1♡
2NT	

- With an unbalanced hand, jump shift. This is unconditionally forcing to game.

♠ A K J 4 3	HCP = 18
♡ 4	Dist. = __
◇ A Q 3 2	Total = __
♣ A 4 3	Unbalanced

You	**Partner**
1♠	1NT
3◇	

Partner must be wary that you may not always have a four-card suit into which you can jump-shift. So in a sequence like

♠ A 3 ♡ A K J 7 5 4 ◇ A Q 2 ♣ 4 3

You	**Partner**
1♡	1♠
3◇	4◇
4♡	

you may very well, as here, have six hearts and only three diamonds — but a rebid of 3♡ by you would not have been forcing.

3. NOTRUMP BIDDING

The rules for opening bids or rebids in notrump are quite simple:

1. Your shape must be 4333, 4432, or 5332 (a balanced hand)
2. Count high card points only — nothing for distribution

NOTRUMP OPENINGS

15-17 HCP	Open 1NT
♠ K Q 2	
♡ A 7	15 HCP
◇ J 10 6 4	
♣ K Q 8 2	

20-21 HCP	Open 2NT
♠ K Q 2	
♡ A 7	20 HCP
◇ K Q J 6 4	
♣ K Q 8	

25-27 HCP	Open 3NT
♠ A Q 2	
♡ A 7	25 HCP
◇ K Q J 6 4	
♣ A K Q	

NOTRUMP REBIDS

12-14 HCP (balanced): Open 1 of a suit and rebid NT if you cannot support partner's suit

	You	*Partner*
♠ A 5	1◇	1♠
♡ A 7 3 2	1NT	
◇ K 9 8 6		
♣ K 9 8		

Always make the most descriptive rebid that you can on a minimum hand. Here if partner were to bid 1♡ over 1◇, since you can support partner, you should do so by bidding 2♡. When partner bids 1♠, rather than 1♡, though, your correct rebid is 1NT.

| *18-19 HCP* | *Open 1 of a suit then jump in NT* | |

♠ A 5 2
♡ A 7
◇ K Q 8 6 4
♣ K Q 8

	You	*Partner*
	1◇	1♡
	2NT	

or, if partner bids at the two-level:

♠ A 5 2
♡ A 7
◇ K Q 8 6 4
♣ K Q 8

	You	*Partner*
	1◇	2♣
	3NT	

| *22-24 HCP* | *Open 2♣ then rebid 2NT (see p.35)* | |

♠ A 5 2
♡ A 7
◇ A K Q 8 6
♣ K Q 8

	You	*Partner*
	2♣	2◇
	2NT	

RESPONDING TO A 1NT OPENING

Once partner has shown a good balanced hand by opening 1NT, the most likely places to play are notrump or a major suit. We therefore divide responder's possible hands as follows:

1. Balanced, with no four-card or longer major

2. Others.

Balanced hand responses to 1NT

On the first type, we are going to play in notrump — we shall decide how high to play (partscore, game or slam) by adding our high-card points to partner's 15-17, giving a bonus point for a 5-card suit headed by the ace or king. Remember:

25 HCP	makes 3NT
33 HCP	makes 6NT
37 HCP	makes 7NT

If you have decided to play in notrump, count only HCP and 1 bonus point for a good five-card suit.

Responding to 1NT on a balanced hand

0-7 HCP	Pass
8-9 HCP	2NT — partner is asked to bid 3NT with 17, and otherwise to pass
10-15 HCP	3NT
16-17 HCP	4NT — partner is asked to bid 6NT with 17, and otherwise to pass
18-19 HCP	6NT
20-21 HCP	5NT — partner is asked to bid 7NT with 17, and otherwise to bid 6NT*
22+ HCP	7NT

*Notice that in this one case, partner does not pass opposite your invitation with less than a maximum hand — your 5NT bid is *forcing*: partner must either bid 6NT or 7NT over it.

Here are some examples of how you respond to a 1NT opening with a balanced hand which does not include a four-card or longer major suit.

6 HCP, balanced

Partner	You
1NT	pass

♠ K Q 4
♡ J 10 6
◊ 7 5 3 2
♣ 9 7 2

9 HCP, balanced

Partner	You
1NT	2NT

♠ K Q 4
♡ Q 10 6
◊ Q 5 3 2
♣ 9 7 2

11 HCP, balanced

Partner	You
1NT	3NT

♠ K Q 4
♡ K 10 6
◊ Q J 3 2
♣ 9 7 2

15 HCP, balanced

Partner	You
1NT	3NT

♠ K Q 4
♡ A J 10
◊ A J 5
♣ 9 7 3 2

Good as this hand is, it is still not enough for slam!

16 HCP, balanced

Partner	**You**
1NT	4NT

♠ K Q 4
♡ J 10 6
◇ A K 3 2
♣ K 7 2

Partner will bid 6NT with a maximum.

18 HCP, balanced

Partner	**You**
1NT	6NT

♠ K Q 4
♡ J 10 6
◇ A K Q 2
♣ K 7 2

Enough for six but not for seven.

20 HCP, balanced

Partner	**You**
1NT	5NT

♠ K Q 4
♡ Q 10 6
◇ A K Q 2
♣ K J 2

Partner will bid 6NT or 7NT.

23 HCP, balanced

Partner	**You**
1NT	7NT

♠ K Q 4
♡ K Q 6
◇ A K Q 2
♣ K J 2

We hope you're playing for money!

Responding to 1NT on other hands

So far, bidding after a 1NT opening has been straightforward — we gave you a balanced hand, so you basically could just count HCP and decide how high to bid. You were always going to play the hand in notrump.

If partner opens 1NT and you have an unbalanced hand, you probably do not want to play in notrump. If your hand contains a four- or five-card major suit, you may still eventually end up in notrump, but you want at least to check out whether four of a major isn't a better or safer contract. You need, therefore, to be able to do a number of things:

- Play in two of a suit with a weak unbalanced hand
- Invite to game, or force to game, while giving partner a choice between your 5-card major and notrump
- Insist on game in your major suit
- Explore for a 4-4 major-suit fit before settling for notrump.

In order to make it easier to handle these auctions, most people play two **conventions**. These are bids to which a special artificial meaning has been assigned, since it is more useful than the natural meaning.

The Stayman Convention

Perhaps the most commonly played convention in all of bridge is the Stayman 2♣ convention, which is used in response to a 1NT opening bid.

Partner	You
1NT	2♣

If you and your partner have agreed to play Stayman (and most of the world does), your 2♣ bid has nothing to do with clubs, but asks the opening bidder to bid a four-card major if she has one. By this means it is possible to find out if you have an eight-card major-suit fit. This is important because when you and your partner have such a fit, you can usually make more tricks playing in the major suit than you can in a notrump contract.

When to use Stayman

Responder's hand must meet the following requirements to make using Stayman worthwhile:

- 8 or more HCP
- at least one 4-card major
- *a short suit — singleton, doubleton or void.*

When you have a short suit, it is safer to play the hand in a trump contract rather than in notrump. A typical hand for a Stayman response to 1NT would be:

♠ J 8 6 3   ♡ 4 2   ◇ A K Q 7   ♣ 7 6 3

Responding to Stayman

Opener has three possible rebids over a Stayman 2♣:

2◇	No four-card major
2♡	I have four hearts, and may have four spades also
2♠	I have four spades and I do not have four hearts

How do you use Stayman?

The addition of Stayman to your bidding arsenal allows you some options on hands where you are interested in at least inviting partner to bid a game, and want to check for a 4-4 major-suit fit. Once you have found a fit, you can count distributional points too, but without a fit, if you are going to play notrump, you may still only count high-card points. Here are some examples of how it works.

Partner	You	♠ K Q 4
1NT	2♣	♡ Q J 5 2
2♡	4♡	◇ K 6 4 2
		♣ 4 3

Having found your 4-4 heart fit, you simply raise to game.

Partner	You	♠ K Q 4
1NT	2♣	♡ J 7 5 2
2♡	3♡	◇ Q 6 4 2
		♣ 4 3

On this hand, you want to play in 4♡ only if partner has more than a minimum.

Partner	You	♠ K Q 4 2
1NT	2♣	♡ Q 7 5
2♡	2NT	◇ Q 6 4 2
		♣ 4 3

Having failed to find a major-suit fit, your 9-HCP hand is worth only an invitation in notrump. Notice that you do not have to bid your spades — since you used Stayman and didn't raise hearts, partner knows by inference you must have four spades.

Partner	You	♠ J 6 4 2
1NT	2♣	♡ A K Q
2♡	3NT	◇ 7 6 4 2
		♣ 4 3

Those hearts may look like a 4-card suit, but they're not! Bid notrump, don't raise hearts.

Partner	You	♠ J 6 4 2
1NT	3NT	♡ A K Q
		◇ 6 4 2
		♣ 4 3 2

Do not use Stayman on a hand with no short suit; just play in notrump.

Hands with a six-card or longer major

These are best handled by using another convention — the **Jacoby Transfer**. This replaces the natural meanings of the 2♦ and 2♡ responses to 1NT and uses them to force opener to bid the next suit up.

	Partner	**You**
	1NT	2♦
	2♡ *(forced)*	
or	1NT	2♡
	2♠ *(forced)*	

There are two advantages of transferring on these hands: the strong hand will be declarer and will be concealed, and the opening lead will come round to it — often worth a trick in itself. Since partner must have at least two cards in your major for the 1NT bid, your choices after transferring are:

0-5 HCP	Pass
6-7 HCP	Raise to three of your major
8-10 HCP	Bid game in your major

5 HCP

Partner	**You**	♠ K Q 6 5 4 2
1NT	2♡	♡ 9 7 5
2♠	pass	◇ 7 6 4
		♣ 4

0 HCP

Partner	**You**	♠ 4 3 2
1NT	2♦	♡ 8 7 6 5 4 2
2♡	pass	◇ 7 6 4
		♣ 4

6 HCP

Partner	**You**	♠ K Q 6 5 4 2
1NT	2♡	♡ J 7 5
2♠	3♠	◇ 7 6 4
		♣ 4

10 HCP

Partner	**You**	♠ K Q 6 5 4 2
1NT	2♡	♡ A 7 5
2♠	4♠	◇ J 6 4
		♣ 4

8 HCP

Partner	**You**	♠ K Q 4
1NT	2♦	♡ 8 7 6 5 4 3
2♡	4♡	◇ K 2
		♣ 3 2

With exactly five cards in your major suit

With weak hands (0-7 HCP), again you will use a transfer to stop in two of your suit (which will likely be a much happier contract than 1NT). However, with invitational or game-going hands, you can offer partner the choice between playing in your major and playing in notrump. Look at these auctions:

Partner	You	♠ K J 6
1NT	2◇	♡ A 9 7 6 3
2♡	2NT	◇ 6 3
		♣ 8 4 2

You have an invitational hand (9 counting your 5-card suit) with five hearts. Partner may pass, bid 3♡, go on to 3NT, or bid 4♡ with a maximum hand and three or more hearts.

Partner	You	♠ K J 6 4 3
1NT	2♡	♡ A 5 2
2♠	3NT	◇ Q 6 2
		♣ 7 6

You have a game-going hand (11+) with five spades. Partner may pass or convert to 4♠.

8 HCP		♠ A 4 3
Partner	You	♡ K 8 6 5 4
1NT	2◇	◇ J 6 4
2♡	2NT	♣ 4 2

Partner can pass 2NT, or convert to 3♡ with three or more hearts. With a maximum he will choose between 3NT and 4♡.

3 HCP		♠ K 8 6 5 4
Partner	You	♡ 9 7
1NT	2♡	◇ 7 6 4 2
2♠	pass	♣ 4 2

11 HCP		♠ K Q 6 5 4
Partner	You	♡ A J 5
1NT	2♡	◇ J 6 4
2♠	3NT	♣ 4 2

Partner can pass 3NT, or convert to 4♠ with three or more spades.

RESPONSES TO 1NT - SUMMARY

Balanced hand, no major suit

0-7 HCP	Pass
8-9 HCP	2NT[1]
10-15 HCP	3NT
16-17 HCP	4NT[1]
18-19 HCP	6NT
20-21 HCP	5NT[2]
22+ HCP	7NT

1. Invitational.
2. Invitational but forcing.

Four-card major suit and a short suit

0-7 HCP	Pass
8-9 HCP	2♣, then 2NT or raise partner to the three-level with a fit
10+ HCP	2♣, then 3NT or raise partner to game with a fit

Five-card major suit

0-7 HCP	Transfer then pass
8-9 HCP	Transfer then 2NT — partner will pass, bid 3NT, or bid 3 or 4 of your major
10+ HCP	Transfer then 3NT — partner will pass or bid 4 of your major

Six-card or longer major suit

0-5 HCP	Transfer then pass
6-7 HCP	Transfer then raise one level. Partner may pass or bid game in your major.
8-14 HCP	Transfer then raise to game in your major.

There is another convention which you may want to learn about, called a Texas transfer, which extends the usefulness of transfers over a 1NT opening bid. It can be played along with Stayman and Jacoby, and allows you to introduce some more complex possibilities into these auctions if you wish. For more on this, see *25 Bridge Conventions You Should Know* (Master Point Press).

RESPONDING TO 2NT OPENINGS

When partner has a powerhouse (20-21 HCP in this case), slam as well as game enters the picture (you need 33 combined HCP for 6NT). Responder's bids are similar to those over 1NT — just add your side's points! This time 3♣ is Stayman, and 3◇ and 3♡ are Jacoby Transfers.

Balanced hand, no major suit

0-3 HCP	Pass
4-10 HCP	3NT
11-12 HCP	4NT[1]
13-14 HCP	6NT
15-16 HCP	5NT[2]
17+ HCP	7NT

1. Invitational to slam.
2. Invitational but forcing.

As you'll see on p.38, the auctions after a 2♣ opening with a 2NT rebid are exactly the same as these — just a slightly different point range.

Four-card major suit

0-3 HCP	Pass
4-10 HCP	3♣ (Stayman), then bid 3NT or game in opener's major with a fit
11+ HCP	3♣, then bid notrump or raise partner to a small slam with a fit

Five-card major suit

0-3 HCP	Transfer then pass
4-10 HCP	Transfer then bid 3NT — partner will pass or bid four of your major
11+ HCP	Transfer then bid at least 4NT

Six-card or longer major suit

0-3 pts.	Transfer then pass
4-10 pts.	Transfer then bid four of your major.
11+ pts.	Transfer then invite to slam in your major

3 HCP		♠ K 6 5 4
Partner	*You*	♡ 9 7 5
2NT	pass	♦ 7 6 4
		♣ 4 3 2

Yes, you are allowed to pass! Even opposite 21, 3 HCP isn't enough to make 3NT, so pass and hope partner can make eight tricks.

0 HCP		♠ 4 3 2
Partner	*You*	♡ 8 7 6 5 4 2
2NT	3♦	♦ 7 6 4
3♡	pass	♣ 4

Again, you have little or nothing to offer, even opposite a bushel of high cards. Transfer to your six-card suit, and hope partner can scramble nine tricks.

6 HCP		♠ K 6 5 4
Partner	*You*	♡ K 7 5 2
2NT	3♣	♦ 7 6 4
3♡	4♡	♣ 4 3

A straightforward Stayman auction.

8 HCP		♠ K Q 6 5 4 2
Partner	*You*	♡ K 7 5
2NT	3♡	♦ 7 6 4
3♠	4♠	♣ 4

You know you have enough for game and not slam, and you also know you have at least a 6-2 spade fit. So transfer to spades and raise partner to 4♠. Sometimes bridge is an easy game!

6 HCP		♠ K Q 6 5
Partner	*You*	♡ 9 7
2NT	3♣	♦ J 6 4
3♠	4♠	♣ 5 4 3 2

Again, what could be simpler? You are going to play 4♠ or 3NT, so check to see whether partner has spades by bidding 3♣ (Stayman). Partner obliges, so you play 4♠.

If you want to play Texas transfers (see p. 33) over a 2NT opening as well as over a 1NT opening, you can certainly do so.

6 HCP	
Partner	*You*
2NT	3♣
3♡	3NT
4♠	

♠ K Q 6 5
♡ 9 7
◇ J 6 4
♣ 5 4 3 2

This time partner isn't quite so cooperative, and bids 3♡ over your 3♣. No problem — you sign off in 3NT. Partner has four spades as well as four hearts, so she converts to 4♠ knowing you would not have bid 3♣ without at least one four-card major.

12 HCP	
Partner	*You*
2NT	4NT

♠ K 3 2
♡ Q 5 4
◇ A 6 4 2
♣ K 4 2

With two balanced hands, a notrump contract is indicated, so count your points to see how high you can go. Your 4NT invites partner to bid 6NT with a maximum 2NT opener.

14 HCP	
Partner	*You*
2NT	6NT

♠ K 3 2
♡ K J 4
◇ A 6 4 2
♣ K 4 2

Again, you want to play in notrump. On this hand, you know you have enough for 6NT between you, but cannot have the 37 HCP necessary for the grand slam. Just raise partner to 6NT.

17 HCP	
Partner	*You*
2NT	7NT

♠ K J 2
♡ K J 4
◇ A Q 6 4
♣ K 4 2

Finally, the hand you have been waiting for all your life. You have a good 1NT opener, and partner opens 2NT! Bid 7NT confidently, and stand by to count up your winnings.

4. REALLY BIG HANDS

Some hands are just too strong to open at the one-level — partner would pass on a hand good enough for you to make game! Any hand of this type is opened with a **Strong 2♣** bid — the only opening bid which partner is not allowed to pass. *This bid has nothing to do with clubs — it just shows a very strong hand.* If you have one of the following, open 2♣ and then bid your real suit when it is your turn to bid again:

> *25+ points and a 5-card suit*
> *23+ points and a 6-card suit*
>   *(or two 5-card suits)*
> *21+ points and a 7-card suit*

Balanced hands too strong to open 2NT also start with 2♣, then rebid notrump:

22-24 HCP	*Open 2♣, rebid 2NT*
28+ HCP	*Open 2♣, rebid 3NT*

♠ A K Q 6 5 4   HCP = 21
♡ A J 5   Dist. = __
♢ A K 4   Total = __
♣ 4

Open 2♣ and rebid spades

♠ A K Q 6 5   HCP = 24
♡ A K J 5   Dist. = __
♢ A K 4   Total = __
♣ 4

Open 2♣ and rebid spades

♠ A 6 4   HCP = 18
♡ A K Q 6 5 4 2   Dist. = __
♢ A J 5   Total = __
♣ —

Open 2♣ and rebid hearts

♠ A K Q 6   HCP = 24
♡ A J 5   Dist. = __
♢ A K J 4   Total = __
♣ Q 4

Open 2♣ and rebid 2NT

RESPONDING TO 2♣ OPENINGS

The only rule when partner opens 2♣ is the following: *you must keep bidding until a game is reached, even if you have 0 points!* There is one exception (you knew we were going to say that, didn't you!): if partner rebids 2NT, showing 22-24 HCP, you are allowed to pass with 0 HCP. In all other cases, you have to bid something. But what?

Partner	You
2♣	2♦

With 0-7 HCP, make an immediate 2♦ 'negative' bid over the 2♣ opening. With 8 or more HCP, bid naturally — your own suit if it is at least five cards long, or notrump.

Partner	You
2♣	2♠

You show at least five spades, and at least 8 pts.

Partner	You
2♣	2NT

This promises 8-10 HCP, and denies a five-card suit of your own.

Partner	You
2♣	3NT

This promises 11+ HCP, and denies a five-card suit of your own.

Once you know what partner's real suit is, you should give priority to raising if you possibly can, even after a negative 2♦ start — remember, partner knows you have less than 8 once you bid 2♦!

Partner	You
2♣	2♦
2♠	3♠

You have three spades, but fewer than 8 pts.

There is another useful convention you can play here, called a 2♦ 'waiting' response to 2♣ (see *25 Bridge Conventions You Should Know*, Master Point Press).

3 HCP		♠ K 6 5 4
Partner	*You*	♡ 9 7 5
2♣	2♢	♢ 7 6 4
2NT	3NT	♣ 4 3 2

Partner's balanced 22-24 plus your 3 is enough to bid game. 2NT is the one rebid you're allowed to pass, but you wouldn't want to with this hand. Notice that with no short suit, you do not bother with Stayman.

0 HCP		♠ 4 3 2
Partner	*You*	♡ 8 7 6 5 4 2
2♣	2♢	♢ 7 6 4
2NT	3♢[1]	♣ 4
3♡	pass	

1. Transfer.

Even opposite partner's huge hand, you have little to offer. Transfer to your suit and drop this auction like a hot potato! On a bad day, partner will have trouble making even nine tricks.

8 HCP		♠ K Q 6 5 4 2
Partner	*You*	♡ K 7 5
2♣	2♠	♢ 7 6 4
3♡	4♡	♣ 4

You have enough to make a positive response, so bid your good six-card suit. With good support for partner's hearts, you raise happily once you hear about them. Partner may very well bid again and you could easily be on for a slam with this hand.

6 HCP		♠ K Q 6 5
Partner	*You*	♡ 9 7
2♣	2♢	♢ J 6 4
2NT	3♣[1]	♣ 5 4 3 2
3♠	4♠	

1. Stayman.

As soon as you hear partner's rebid, you know you are going to play this hand in 4♠ or 3NT. Having found the fit, you simply bid game. Partner has described his hand and will respect your decision not to go any higher.

6 HCP		♠ K Q 6 5
Partner	**You**	♡ 9 7
2♣	2♢	♢ J 6 4
2NT	3♣[1]	♣ 5 4 3 2
3♡	3NT	

1. Stayman.

The same auction as the last example, but partner bids hearts. Sign off in 3NT — if partner has spades as well, she will convert to 4♠ (you wouldn't go through Stayman unless you owned a four-card major…).

10 HCP		♠ K 3 2
Partner	**You**	♡ 6 5 4 2
2♣	2NT	♢ A 6 4
3♠	4♠	♣ K 4 2

With a balanced 10 HCP, you bid 2NT first time around, to describe a balanced 8-10, then raise partner's suit once you find out what it is. Again, partner will probably bid on, as the two hands are well in the slam range.

12 HCP		♠ K 3 2
Partner	**You**	♡ K J 4 2
2♣	3NT	♢ A 6 4
6NT		♣ J 6 2

With a balanced 12 HCP, you have another simple descriptive bid available: 3NT showing 11+. Partner picks the final contract; presumably he has a notrump hand himself.

1 HCP		♠ 4 3 2
Partner	**You**	♡ J 4 2
2♣	2♢	♢ 8 6 4
2♡	4♡	♣ 7 6 4 2

You would dearly love to pass 2♡, but you're not allowed to (at least, not if you ever want to play with this partner again!). Since you're forced to game, get the agony over with and bid 4♡ right away, saying 'Partner, I hate my hand — but I do like hearts.'

5. WEAK HANDS

No, it's not your imagination: you really do hold many more very poor hands than very strong hands. However, that doesn't mean you can't get into the bidding. With the exception of 2♣, opening bids at the two- and three-levels are reserved to show weak hands with a single long suit. The purpose of these openings is to be *pre-emptive* — you are trying to take up bidding space and make it difficult for the opponents to find their best contract.

WEAK TWO-BIDS

An opening bid of 2◊, 2♡ or 2♠ shows a very specific hand:

> *Exactly a 6-card suit*
> *6-10 HCP*
> *2 of the top 3 honors (or 3 of the top 5)*
> *in your suit*

It is important to stick to these rules, since your partner may have quite a good hand when you open a weak two-bid.

♠ A K 8 6 5 4
♡ 9 7   7 *HCP*
◊ 7 6 4
♣ 4 3

A textbook 2♠ opener.

♠ K 8 6 4 3 2
♡ A 2   7 *HCP*
◊ 7 6 4
♣ 4 3

Pass this hand — the suit does not qualify under our rules (only 1 of the top 3 or 5 honors).

♠ A K 8 6 4 3 2
♡ 2   7 *HCP*
◊ 7 6 4
♣ 4 3

Don't open 2♠ with this hand — the suit does not qualify under our rules (must be exactly a 6-card suit). You'll see what to do with this hand on page 43.

41

Responding to Weak Twos

When partner opens a weak two-bid (2♠, for the sake of example), you have several options:

- With a poorish hand and 3 trumps, raise to make it harder for the opponents.

7 HCP	♠ K 8 6
Dist. __	♡ A 2
Total __	◇ 7 6 4 2
	♣ 9 8 4 3

Partner	You
2♠	3♠

- With a poorish hand and 4 trumps, double raise to make it really tough for the opponents.

7 HCP	♠ K 8 6 3
Dist. __	♡ A 2
Total __	◇ 7 6 4
	♣ 9 8 4 3

Partner	You
2♠	4♠

- With a good hand and trump support, raise to game and expect to make it.

14 HCP	♠ K 8 6 3
Dist. __	♡ A 2
Total __	◇ A K 4
	♣ 9 8 4 3

Partner	You
2♠	4♠

- If you're unsure where to play the hand, bid 2NT asking partner to bid a feature (an ace or king outside his suit), then decide.

15 HCP	♠ K 8
Dist. __	♡ A Q 5 2
Total __	◇ A Q 4
	♣ 9 8 4 3

Partner	You
2♠	2NT
3♣	3NT

Lacking trump support and with a less than stellar hand, just pass partner's bid and hope it damages the opposition more than it does you!

HIGHER-LEVEL PREEMPTS

Remember this hand from p.41?

♠ A K 8 6 4 3 2
♡ 2
♢ 7 6 4
♣ 4 3

We said you couldn't open 2♠ because you have a 7-card suit — but you can actually do even better: you can open 3♠! The principle is the same, but you are raising the barrage a level higher. You are also taking more of a risk that they will simply double you and extract a large penalty. Three-level openings are typically made on weak hands with a long suit:

> *10 or fewer HCP*
> *A quality 7-card suit*

A good rule to use is the **Rule of 2 and 3** — not vulnerable, you expect to go down three tricks, vulnerable you expect to go down two. Then, if they double you, the penalty will be no more than 500.

With an even longer suit you can even open at the four-level, still keeping the Rule of 2 and 3 in mind.

♠ A K 9 8 6 4 3 2
♡ 2
♢ 7 6
♣ 4 3

With an eight-card suit this time, you expect to make 7 or 8 tricks in your own hand. You should open 4♠ on this hand — anything less would simply be too wimpy for words!

In summary

- *You should have 10 or fewer HCP to open a preempt*
- *With a good 6-card suit, use a weak 2-bid*
- *With a good 7-card suit, open at the 3-level*
- *With a good 8-card suit, open at the 4-level*

♠ K Q J 10 9 8 7
♡ 2   *6 HCP*
◇ 7 6 5 4
♣ 4

Does the idea of opening 3♠ with this hand scare you? It shouldn't. You have six certain tricks despite your lack of high cards.

♠ J 10 9 8 7 6 5
♡ K 5   *10 HCP*
◇ A Q 4
♣ 4

This hand is just too good for a preempt. Partner will expect you to have a better suit and fewer high cards outside it. Add your points, and you'll find this hand qualifies as a 1♠ opening!

♠ 9 7 6 5 4 3 2
♡ K Q J 5   *5 HCP*
◇ 6 4
♣ —

On this hand, your suit is very poor, while you don't mind if they want to play in hearts. Just pass, and wait for them to get into trouble.

RESPONDING TO PREEMPTS

Usually, passing is correct, but there are exceptions:

12 HCP	♠ 3 2
Dist. __	♡ A K 2
Total __	◇ A J 6 4
	♣ 7 6 4 3

| **Partner** | **You** |
| 3♠ | 4♠ |

You could raise a vulnerable partner to game with this hand — he promises seven tricks, while you have three plus a couple of trumps.

17 HCP	♠ A K J 10 2
Dist. __	♡ 2
Total __	◇ A K 4
	♣ Q 6 4 3

| **Partner** | **You** |
| 3♡ | 3♠ |

Your hand is so good, it is worth bidding your own 5-card suit (forcing). Perhaps partner has three spades...

6. CONVENTIONS

You have already encountered examples of conventions — bids that by agreement have a completely artificial meaning, like the Stayman 2♣ which enquires about 4-card majors. Literally thousands of conventions have been invented, and you will undoubtedly learn and play some of them in your bridge career. One you must know, since it is one of the most widely used, and one of the earliest invented, is the **Blackwood** convention, in which a bid of 4NT asks about the number of aces in partner's hand. It enables the partnership to stay out of slam when two aces are missing. *Notice that a 4NT bid is only Blackwood when a trump suit has been agreed, either directly or by implication. In all other cases, it is a natural notrump bid.* Thus:

| 1♠ | 3♠ | |
| 4NT | | *Blackwood* |

| 1NT | 4NT | *natural* |

THE BLACKWOOD CONVENTION

Over a Blackwood 4NT, responder makes one of the following replies:

0 or 4 aces	5♣
1 ace	5♦
2 aces	5♡
3 aces	5♠

A 5NT continuation confirms that all four aces are held, and asks for kings, using the same responses at the 6-level.

1♠	3♠	
4NT	5♦	1 ace (♠ agreed)
5NT	6♡	2 kings

1♠	2♡	
4NT	5♣	0 or 4 aces (♡ agreed)
5♡	6♡	It was 4 aces

| 1♠ | 4NT | |
| 5♦ | 6♠ | 1 ace (♠ agreed) |

7. COMPETITIVE BIDDING

OVERCALLS

When one side has opened the bidding, it is still possible for the other to enter the auction as an opponent. One way in which you can compete in the bidding is by making an **overcall**.

Oppt.	You	Oppt.	Partner
1♣	1♠		

This is a **simple overcall** — you have bid your own suit at the lowest possible level. This shows

8-17 points
at least a good 5-card suit

On the above auction, you could have either of the two hands shown here:

♠ A K J 10 2 ♡ 2 ◇ A 5 4 ♣ Q 6 4 3
♠ A K J 10 2 ♡ 2 ◇ 9 8 4 ♣ 7 6 4 3

You should not overcall 1♠ with either of the next two examples, though:

♠ Q 6 4 3 2 ♡ 2 ◇ A 5 4 ♣ Q 6 4 3
♠ K Q J 3 2 ♡ 4 2 ◇ 9 8 4 ♣ 7 6 4

Do not overcall 1♠ with either of these hands. The suit is too weak in the first case, and the whole hand is too weak in the second.

♠ Q 6 4 3 2 ♡ 2 ◇ A K 5 4 ♣ Q 6 4
♠ K Q J 10 2 ♡ 4 2 ◇ Q 8 4 ♣ 7 6 4

Now the first hand is strong enough to overcall 1♠, despite the weak spade suit. The good spades in the second case make up for the lack of high cards, so again, overcall 1♠ if they open.

♠ 6 4 3 ♡ 2 ◇ 6 5 4 ♣ A K 10 9 8 3
♠ J 6 4 3 ♡ 2 ◇ K 8 4 ♣ A K J 10 3

If the auction forces you to make an overcall at the two-level, you must have at least 10 HCP. The first of these hands is too weak to make a 2♣ overcall. The second hand has enough high cards to qualify.

RESPONDING TO OVERCALLS

With trump support, the responses to an overcall are similar to responses to an opening bid, with due allowance for the fact that the overcaller may have far fewer high cards than he would need to open.

8 HCP

♠ J 10 2 ♡ 3 2 ◇ A J 4 2 ♣ Q 6 4 3

Oppt.	Partner	Oppt.	You
1♣	1♠	pass	2♠

With 8-11 points and three trumps, raise one level.

11 HCP

♠ J 10 2 ♡ K 2 ◇ A J 4 2 ♣ Q 6 4 3

Oppt.	Partner	Oppt.	You
1♣	1♠	pass	3♠

With 12-14 points and three trumps, raise two levels.

14 HCP

♠ J 10 2 ♡ K 2 ◇ A Q 4 2 ♣ A 6 4 3

Oppt.	Partner	Oppt.	You
1♣	1♠	pass	4♠

With 15+ points and trump support, raise three levels.

11 HCP

♠ 3 2 ♡ A Q J 4 2 ◇ 10 4 ♣ A 6 4 3

Oppt.	Partner	Oppt.	You
1♣	1♠	pass	2♡

With 10+ points but no trump support, you may bid your own good 5+-card suit. Unless you are a passed hand, this bid is forcing — partner will have to respond. Be careful here; since partner has to bid, in the auction shown he does not promise six spades if he rebids 2♠.

Notrump responses to overcalls

As always, notrump bids show specific point count ranges. This time, they also show stoppers in the suit the opponents have bid, and deny three or more cards in partner's suit.

9 HCP

♠ 3 2   ♡ A J 4 2   ◇ 10 4 2   ♣ A 6 4 3

Oppt.	Partner	Oppt.	You
1♣	1♠	pass	1NT

This shows 8-11 HCP and one stopper.

13 HCP

♠ 3 2   ♡ A J 4 2   ◇ K 4 2   ♣ A J 4 3

Oppt.	Partner	Oppt.	You
1♣	1♠	pass	2NT

This shows 12-14 HCP and 1½ stoppers.

15 HCP

♠ 3 2   ♡ A J 4 2   ◇ K Q 2   ♣ A J 4 3

Oppt.	Partner	Oppt.	You
1♣	1♠	pass	3NT

This shows 15+ HCP and 1½ stoppers.

Summary of responses to overcalls		
With three trumps		
8-11 points	raise one level	
12-14 points	raise two levels	
15+ points	raise three levels	
With a balanced hand, bid notrump		
8-11 HCP, 1 stopper	cheapest NT bid	
12-14 HCP, 1½ stoppers	jump in NT	
15+ HCP, 1½ stoppers	bid 3NT	
With 10+ HCP and a good 5-card suit		
Bid your own suit (forcing one round)		

OVERCALLING 1NT
15 HCP

♠ 3 2 ♥ A J 4 2 ♦ K Q 2 ♣ A J 4 3

Oppt.	Partner	Oppt.	You
1♣			1NT

This overcall very specifically shows the same hand as an opening 1NT bid (15-17 HCP), but in addition, it promises 1½ stoppers in the opponents' suit.

The simplest way to continue the auction is to bid as though partner had opened 1NT. This is Stayman:

Oppt.	Partner	Oppt.	You
1♣	1NT	pass	2♣

and this is a transfer to spades:

Oppt.	Partner	Oppt.	You
1♣	1NT	pass	2♥

JUMP OVERCALLS

Oppt.	You	Oppt.	Partner
1♣	2♥		

Oppt.	You	Oppt.	Partner
1♠	3♦		

In each of these auctions you have bid your suit a level higher than was necessary.

These are preemptive (weak) bids, and correspond to opening bids at the two- and three-levels. Partner will expect you to have a weak hand (10 or fewer HCP) and a good long suit. At the two-level, the requirements are the same as for a weak two-bid opening: a six-card suit containing two of the top three or three of the top five honors. At the three-level, you need a decent seven-card suit.

> Just as is the case with preemptive openings, you need to pay attention to the vulnerability (in case someone decides to double you). The Rule of 2 and 3 mentioned earlier (page 43) is useful here too.

TAKEOUT DOUBLES

Sometimes you will have a decent hand (13+ points) but cannot overcall because your hand does not fit the rules we described in the previous section. Perhaps you do not have a 5-card suit, for example, while your hand does not qualify for a 1NT overcall. You may, however, be able to make a **takeout double**, asking partner to bid her own best suit.

*Any double of a suit bid made below game, at the doubler's first opportunity, if partner has not bid, is a **takeout double**; all other doubles are for penalty.*

Oppt.	Partner	Oppt.	You
		1♣	dbl

Oppt.	Partner	Oppt.	You
		2♠	dbl

Oppt.	Partner	Oppt.	You
1♢	pass	1♠	dbl

All the above are takeout doubles.

To make a takeout double you must have:

- *Adequate trump support for all unbid suits (but see the third point below)*
- *At least an opening bid (13+ points)*

or

- *A very strong hand (17+ points, too good for an overcall). With this kind of hand you start with a double and then bid your own suit.*

♠ 3 ♡ A J 4 2 ◇ K 4 3 2 ♣ A J 4 3

Oppt.	Partner	Oppt.	You
		1♠	dbl

This is a textbook takeout double. Notice that if the opening bid were anything but 1♠, you would not be able to double, since you do not have trump support for spades. Since you do not have a good suit of your own, you would reluctantly have to pass over an opening bid of 1♣, 1♢ or 1♡.

Responses to takeout doubles

With no intervening bid, the doubler's partner *must* respond, even with 0 points. If there is an intervening bid, a response shows at least 8 points, since you are no longer forced to bid.

With no intervening bid:	
0-8 points	Bid your longest suit at the cheapest level
9-11 points	Jump in your longest suit
12 points	Jump to the three-level in your longest suit
13+ points	With a five-card major, jump to game in that major; otherwise bid the opponent's suit (a **cuebid**) to create a game force.

♠ J 4 3 2   ♡ Q 3 2   ◇ 5 4 3   ♣ 5 4 3

Oppt.	Partner	Oppt.	You
1◇	dbl	pass	1♠

With a minimum hand, bid your spades as cheaply as possible

♠ J 4 3 2   ♡ A 2   ◇ K 4 3   ♣ J 4 3 2

Oppt.	Partner	Oppt.	You
1◇	dbl	pass	2♠

With this hand, jump in spades.

♠ J 5 4 3 2   ♡ A 3   ◇ A K 3   ♣ Q 5 4

Oppt.	Partner	Oppt.	You
1◇	dbl	pass	4♠

With an opening bid of your own and five spades, jump to game here.

♠ J 5 4 3   ♡ A Q 3   ◇ 3 2   ♣ A K 5 4

Oppt.	Partner	Oppt.	You
1◇	dbl	pass	2◇

Game-forcing, 13+ points, no five-card major. The cuebid says nothing about diamonds, but simply forces partner to keep bidding.

Notrump responses to a takeout double

As always, a notrump bid shows a balanced hand and a very specific point range, and this time it promises that you have the opponent's suit stopped too.

9-11 HCP, 1 stopper	1NT
12-14 HCP, 1½ stoppers	2NT
15+ HCP, 1½ stoppers	3NT

Never respond to a takeout double in notrump if you could respond in a major suit.

♠ J 4 3   ♡ A 9 2   ◇ K 4 3   ♣ J 4 3 2

Oppt.	Partner	Oppt.	You
1◇	dbl	pass	1NT

A balanced 9 HCP and a diamond stopper.

♠ Q 5 4   ♡ A 3 2   ◇ K J 3   ♣ Q 5 4 2

Oppt.	Partner	Oppt.	You
1◇	dbl	pass	2NT

A balanced 12 HCP, with your diamond honors counting as 1½ stoppers.

♠ J 5   ♡ A Q 3   ◇ A J 10 2   ♣ A 6 5 4

Oppt.	Partner	Oppt.	You
1◇	dbl	pass	3NT

Balanced, 16 HCP, and diamonds stopped twice: a perfect 3NT response.

♠ 6 5   ♡ A 7 3 2   ◇ K 3 2   ♣ K 6 5 4

Oppt.	Partner	Oppt.	You
1◇	dbl	pass	2♡

Even with 10 HCP balanced and a diamond stopper, you must not conceal your heart suit. You can bid notrump next round, if you want.

♠ K 6 5 2   ♡ A J 7 2   ◇ 6 3   ♣ A 10 4

Oppt.	Partner	Oppt.	You
1◇	dbl	pass	2◇

You are not sure which major to bid, so you pass the buck by bidding the opponent's suit. This is a *cuebid*, forcing partner to bid. Now she will name her major.

8. BALANCING

When a pass by you will end the auction, you are in the **balancing** seat. If the auction is going to die at a low level, you should always think about taking a bid. It is often right to do so on hands where you would not think of bidding in any other situation.

♠ K 8 5 4 ♡ Q 7 6 3 ◇ 6 ♣ A 10 5 2

Oppt.	Partner	Oppt.	You
1◇	pass	pass	?

Your first thought will be to pass; but suppose partner has

♠ 9 3 ♡ A J 10 2 ◇ A 7 4 ♣ K J 7 3

He could do nothing but pass over 1◇, since he is not strong enough to overcall 1NT, while his lack of support for spades makes a takeout double a poor bid. However, if you balance with a takeout double of your own, you will find your 4-4 heart fit and make a lot of tricks!

DECIDING WHEN TO BALANCE

Mentally add 3 points to your hand, and then make the same bid (overcall or make a takeout double) as you would have if the opening bid had been on your right.

In our example, with another 3 points you would have enough to make a takeout double of 1◇ on your right, so it is OK to double 1◇ in balancing seat.

♠ K 8 6 5 2 ♡ 5 ◇ J 7 4 2 ♣ K 3 2

Oppt.	Partner	Oppt.	You
1♡	pass	pass	1♠

Your suit is too poor for a normal overcall, but add 3 points and it is clear to balance.

RESPONDING TO A BALANCING BID

When partner balances, mentally subtract 3 points from your hand, then respond as you would if partner had made an overcall or takeout double directly over the opening bid.

♠ K Q 5 4 2 ♡ 10 8 6 ◇ J 7 2 ♣ 5 2

Oppt.	Partner	Oppt.	You
1♣	pass	pass	?

Mentally give yourself the ♡K instead of the ♡6, and you have an easy 1♠ overcall if 1♣ is bid on your right. That makes it right to overcall 1♠ now in the balancing seat.

♠ K 8 5 ♡ A 6 ◇ A 10 7 6 ♣ K 8 5 2

Oppt.	Partner	Oppt.	You
1◇	pass	pass	?

Add 3 HCP to this hand and you have 17; you are balanced with a diamond stopper. Does that ring a bell? Right, overcall 1NT. In balancing chair, this shows 12-14 HCP, three less than in the direct position (see p. 49)

♠ K Q 5 4 ♡ 7 6 ◇ 8 6 4 ♣ A K J 2

Oppt.	Partner	Oppt.	You
		1◇	pass
pass	dbl	pass	?

Bid 2♠ with this hand. If partner had doubled in direct seat, you would want to play in game, but replace the ♠K with the ♠2, and you are just worth a jump. Partner has already bid 3 of your points, so subtract them before responding.

♠ K 8 5 ♡ Q 7 6 ◇ A J 7 ♣ A 10 5 2

Oppt.	Partner	Oppt.	You
		1◇	pass
pass	dbl	pass	1NT

This is a nice hand; but pretend the ♣A is the ♣J — now what do you think? If you take those 3 points away, you are right in the range for a 1NT response. In fact, 1NT shows 12-14 HCP in response to a balancing double.

> All the rules about overcalls, takeout doubles and their responses still apply in a balancing situation — just remember to add or subtract those 3 points. When balancing, *overbid* by 3 points. When responding, *underbid* by 3 points.

9. DECLARER PLAY

SUIT CONTRACTS

After the opening lead is made and dummy comes down, stop and *count your losers*. If you have too many, make a plan to dispose of them; then decide whether it's safe to draw the opponents' trumps before beginning your project.

1. Ruff losers with dummy's trumps

Declarer	Dummy
♠ K Q J 8 7	♠ A 9 5 4 2
♡ A 8 3	♡ 7
◇ K Q 4	◇ A 7 2
♣ A 4	♣ K 7 3 2

Playing 7♠, you have two losers (in hearts), but after you cash the ♡A dummy will be void in hearts and can ruff your losers. You need only two trumps in dummy for this, so draw trumps, play the ♡A and trump your small hearts in dummy to make your grand slam.

2. Throw losers on dummy's winners

Declarer	Dummy
♠ K Q J 8 7	♠ A 9 5 4
♡ A 8 3	♡ 9 7
◇ K Q 4	◇ A 7 2
♣ A 4	♣ K Q J 2

Playing 7♠, you have two losers (in hearts) again. This time, draw trumps and throw your hearts on dummy's good clubs (playing the ace from the short side first).

3. Make useful discards from dummy

Declarer	Dummy
♠ K Q J 8 7	♠ A 9 5 4 2
♡ 8 3	♡ A 7 4
◇ K 4	◇ A 7 2
♣ A K Q 4	♣ J 2

Playing 7♠, you have one loser (in hearts) this time. Here you must draw trumps and throw dummy's little hearts on your good clubs. Now trump a heart in dummy to make your slam.

4) Take a finesse

Declarer	Dummy
♠ K Q J 8 7	♠ A 9 5 4
♡ 8 3	♡ A Q 4 2
♢ K Q 4	♢ A 7 2
♣ A K Q	♣ J 3

Playing 7♠, you have only one loser (in hearts). This time, draw trumps and lead a heart to the queen. If the king is well placed, the queen will win the trick.

5) Set up dummy's long suit

Declarer	Dummy
♠ K Q J 8 7	♠ A 9 5
♡ 8 3	♡ K Q J 2
♢ K 5 4	♢ A 7 2
♣ A K Q	♣ J 3 2

Playing 6♠, you have two losers (one in hearts and one in diamonds). This time, draw trumps and lead a heart to the king. Later, you will discard a diamond from your hand on dummy's ♡J.

NOTRUMP CONTRACTS

After the opening lead is made and dummy comes down, stop and *count your winners*. If you do not have enough sure tricks without losing the lead, try to develop extra tricks in the suit in which you have most cards in the combined hands. Do not cash your other winners before doing this!

Declarer	Dummy
♠ K 10 8 4	♠ A 9 5
♡ A 8 3	♡ 7 2
♢ K Q 4	♢ A 7 2
♣ J 5 4	♣ K Q 10 6 2

You are playing 3NT and they lead a heart. You have only six sure tricks, and the rest must come from dummy's club suit. *Hold up* the ♡A as long as you can — here, you will win the third round of hearts. Then play clubs. If you are lucky, the opponents will be able to cash only one more heart when they win the ♣A — or if you are even more lucky, the opponent with the ♣A will have no more hearts to lead!

10. OPENING LEADS

AGAINST SUIT CONTRACTS

In order of preference, your leads should be:

1. Partner's bid suit
2. From **A**Kx
   The ace is led from this holding
3. Top of a perfect sequence
   KQJx   **Q**J10x   **J**109x
4. Top of a broken sequence
   KQ10x   **Q**J9x   **J**108x
5. A singleton, hoping for a ruff
6. A suit the opponents have not bid
7. Fourth best from an honor
   K96**2**   Q108**4**2
   However, do not underlead an ace against a suit contract — if declarer or dummy has a singleton, you may never win your ace!
8. Top of nothing
   854   **9**62
9. Top of a small doubleton
   73   **8**2

AGAINST NOTRUMP CONTRACTS

In order of preference, your leads should be:

1. Partner's bid suit
2. Top of a perfect sequence
   KQJx   **Q**J10x   **J**109x
3. Top of a broken sequence
   KQ10x   **Q**J9x   **J**108x
4. Top of an interior sequence
   K**J**10x   Q**10**9x   A**Q**Jx
5. A suit the opponents have not bid
6. Fourth best from your longest and strongest suit
   K96**2**   A108**4**2
7. Top of nothing
   854   **9**62

---

1. These preferred leads hold throughout the hand, not just on opening lead.
2. Remember B.O.S.T.O.N. — **B**ottom **O**f **S**omething, **T**op **O**f **N**othing.

11. USEFUL BRIDGE TERMS

Balancing

Keeping the bidding alive with a bid or double when the opposing bidding has stopped at a low level.

Blackwood

A conventional bid of 4NT after a suit has been agreed, asking partner how many aces she holds. See p. 45.

Convention

A bid which is agreed to have an artificial meaning. The Stayman 2♣ response to 1NT to ask about major-suit holdings is a common example of a convention.

Crossruff

A technique where declarer makes his trumps separately by ruffing one suit in the dummy and another in his hand.

Cuebid

A bid of the opponents' suit, used to create a forcing situation or to show a control in a slam auction. Cuebids can be assigned many conventional meanings.

Dealer

The person who deals the cards (at rubber bridge) and the player with the first turn in the auction (in any form of the game).

Declarer

The first player to bid the denomination of the final contract. If the final contract is 2♠, then the player who first bid spades is declarer. His partner's hand becomes dummy after the opening lead, and declarer controls the play of both hands.

Distributional Points

Points counted for short or long suits in addition to high card points. See p. 4.

Double

A call that in its natural sense offers to increase the penalties if the opponents' contract fails, and the rewards if it makes. Doubles are often used for other purposes (see 'Takeout Double').

Doubleton

A holding of exactly two cards in a suit.

Dummy

The hand belonging to declarer's partner. After the opening lead, the dummy is placed face up on the table, and declarer controls the play from that hand as well as his own.

Dummy Points

Points counted for distribution by a hand expecting to be dummy, after a trump fit has been found. See p. 5.

Finesse

An attempt to win a trick with a card that is not as high as one held by the opponents. The success of a finesse will depend on the position of the opponents' high card.

Forcing

A bid is forcing when the bidder's partner may not pass at his next turn. A bid may be not forcing, forcing for one round, or forcing to game.

Game

A game contract is one worth at least 100 points, which if successful earns a 'game bonus'. The minimum game contracts are 3NT, 4♠, 4♡, 5◇, and 5♣.

Grand slam

A contract to take all thirteen tricks.

High Card Points (HCP)

Points counted for honor cards:

A=4, K=3, Q=2, J=1

Honor

An ace, king, queen or jack (sometimes a 10).

Invitational

An invitational bid asks partner to evaluate his hand and bid on if he has maximum strength for the auction so far.

Jacoby Transfer

A convention used in response to partner's 1NT opening, where a bid of 2♦ requires opener to bid 2♥, and a bid of 2♥ requires opener to bid 2♠. This enables responder to describe a range of hands with a 5- or 6-card major suit, while arranging for the opening lead to come up to the strong hand. Jacoby Transfers can also be used at the 3-level after a 2NT opening.

Jump overcall

An overcall that skips one level of bidding in the auction (e.g. an overcall of 2♦ over an opponent's opening bid of 1♣). Jump overcalls are usually made on weak hands.

Jump raise

A raise of partner's suit that skips one or more levels of bidding (e.g. a raise of partner's 1♠ opening to 3♠).

Jump shift

A new suit response to an opening bid that skips one level of bidding (e.g. a response of 3♦ to partner's 1♠ opening). A jump shift is forcing to game.

Lead

The first card played to a trick.

Limited bid

A limited bid is one which defines the bidder's point range (for example, an opening 1NT bid). Many limited bids are not forcing, but this is not always the case.

Major Suit

Spades and hearts, worth 30 points per trick for the contract score.

Minor Suit

Clubs and diamonds, worth 20 points per trick for the contract score.

Non-forcing

A non-forcing bid is one which may be passed. An opening 2NT, while strong, is non-forcing.

Notrump

A denomination higher than the four suits. There is no trump suit and no ruffing is possible on a deal played at notrump.

Opener

The first player to make a call in the auction other than pass.

Opening lead

The lead to the first trick, which is made by the player on declarer's left.

Overcall

A bid of a suit or notrump by the side which did not open the bidding.

Overruff

To play a trump to a trick which is of higher value than any trump that has been previously played to the same trick.

Preference

When opener has bid two suits, responder gives preference by passing or returning to the one he likes better.

e.g.   1♡   1♠
         2♣   2♡

Such a bid does not promise more strength than does the initial response.

Point Count

A common hand evaluation method which involves counting High Card Points and Distributional Points.

Preempt (preemptive)

A bid usually made on a poor defensive hand, designed to take up space in the auction and make it hard for the opponents to arrive at their best contract. Opening bids at the 3-level and higher are usually preemptive in nature.

Rebid

A second bid by a player who has already made at least one call.

Redouble

A call available immediately after a double to the side which has been doubled. Ostensibly, this call increases rewards and penalties once again, but like the double itself, a redouble can have a conventional meaning.

Responder

The partner of the opening bidder.

Reverse

A sequence where opener rebids a higher-ranking suit than his first suit, at the 2-level or higher. It promises at least 5-4 shape and 17+ points. See p. 22.

Ruff

To play a trump on a trick where a non-trump suit was led. 'To trump' and 'to ruff' are synonyms.

Rule of 2 and 3

A rule governing when to preempt. The bidder expects to go down two tricks if he is vulnerable or three if he is not vulnerable.

Rule of 20

Add your HCP to the lengths of your two longest suits; if you get 20 or more, you may open the bidding.

Singleton

A holding of exactly one card in a suit.

Slam

A contract for twelve or thirteen tricks.

Small slam

A contract for twelve tricks.

Stayman

A conventional 2♣ response to an opening 1NT, asking opener whether he has a four-card major.

Takeout double

A convention whereby a double is used to ask partner to bid his best suit. See p. 50.

Tenace

A card holding in the same suit which is not quite in sequence, e.g. A-Q, K-J.

Total Points

High Card Points plus Distributional Points.

Transfer

A bid that requires partner to bid a specific suit, usually the next one higher. See Jacoby Transfer.

Trick

Four cards played one in turn by each player. A complete deal consists of thirteen tricks.

Trump

The suit named by the final contract (unless it is notrump). A player unable to follow suit to a trick may instead play a trump; the highest trump played to a trick wins the trick.

Unlimited Bid

An unlimited bid is one that does not place an upper limit on the strength of one's hand i.e., we know the bottom but we don't know the top. An unlimited bid is always forcing.

Void

A holding of no cards at all in a suit.

Weak two-bid

A preemptive opening made with a good 6-card suit and 6-10 HCP. The hand is not good enough to open one of a suit.

12. SCORING

Trick score (below the line)

♣, ◊	20 per trick
♠, ♡	30 per trick
NT	40 (1st trick), 30 thereafter

Overtricks (above the line)

Undoubled	Trick Value	
	Not Vul.	*Vul.*
Doubled	100	200
Redoubled	200	400

Rubber bonus

2-game rubber	700
3-game rubber	500

Slam Bonus

	Not vul.	*Vul.*
Small slam	500	750
Grand slam	1000	1500

Miscellaneous

Making a doubled contract: 50 for the insult
Making a redoubled contract: 100 for the insult

Penalties for undertricks

Not vulnerable	50 per trick
Doubled	100 (1st), 200 (2nd and 3rd), 300 thereafter
Redoubled	200 (1st), 400 (2nd and 3rd), 600 thereafter
Vulnerable	100 per trick
Doubled	200 1st trick, 300 thereafter
Redoubled	400 1st trick, 600 thereafter

Honors

In the trump suit

Holding 4 honors in one hand	100
Holding 5 honors in one hand	150

At notrump

Holding four aces in one hand	150

DUPLICATE BRIDGE SCORING

As above, except:

- no rubber bonus or honors
- partscore bonus 50
- game bonus of 300 not vul., 500 vul.